THE ABC'S OF CHRISTMAS

Written by
Francine M. O'Connor

Illustrated by
Bartholomew

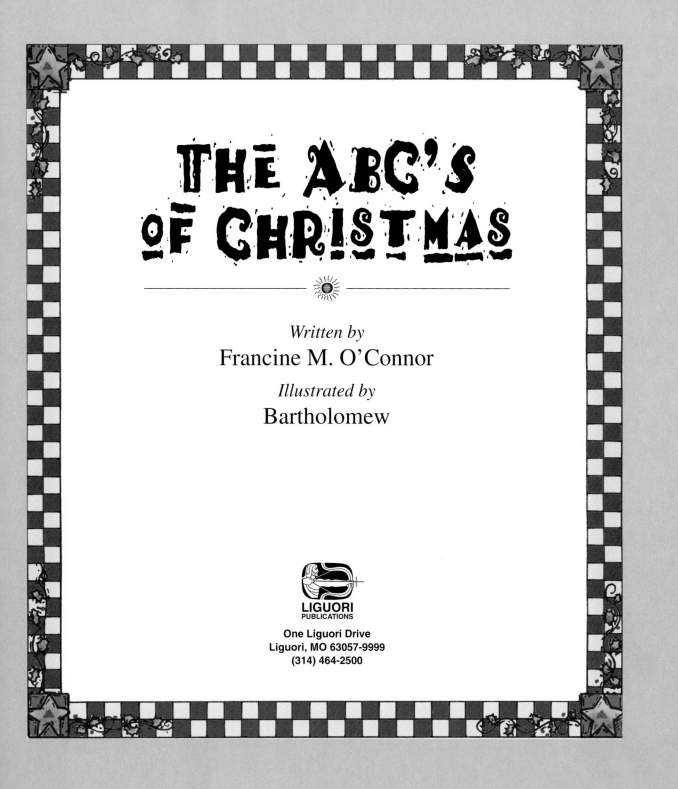

LIGUORI
PUBLICATIONS

One Liguori Drive
Liguori, MO 63057-9999
(314) 464-2500

ISBN 0-89243-581-X
Library of Congress Catalog Card Number: 94-76021

LISTEN TO ISAIAH

Listen to Isaiah,
the man who talked to kings
of God the Father's love and care
and other wondrous things.

"He'll give rain for the seed
that you put in the ground.
The wheat in your fields
will be the finest around."

Listen to Isaiah.
He reminds us once again
of God's promise to send a savior
to save the world from sin.

"Then the deaf will hear
words read from a book.
Out of the gloom and darkness,
the eyes of the blind will look."

Listen to Isaiah.
His words will help us learn
the wonder of that glorious night
when the infant King was born.

"For unto us a child is born
whose reign will never cease.
They'll name him Wonder-Counselor,
God-Hero, Prince of Peace."

Listen to Isaiah,
as God's promise he brings to you.
He places God's love in every soul
and God's peace in hearts that are true.

THE LADY AND THE ANGEL

On a quiet night in Nazareth
God's special angel came to call
on a lady by the name of Mary,
the most beautiful lady of all.

The angel said, "You are blessed, Mary,
for you are the specially chosen one.
Of all the women in the world,
you are asked to bear God's Son."

So Mary became the mother of Jesus;
and when he was just the tiniest boy,
she gave him every bit of her love,
and he gave her such heavenly joy.

She held his hand as he learned to walk
and kissed his bruises when he fell down.
Once when he wandered out of her sight,
she scolded him with a worried frown.

Now Jesus asked Mary to watch over us,
for he knows how well she understands
about bumps and bruises and broken toys
and temper tantrums and sticky hands.

And because it's lonely to be so small
in a world that seems so large,
God sends us angels from heaven
to keep us in their loving charge.

LITTLE DONKEY'S TALE

Ninety miles to Bethlehem,
"Come, little donkey, we must go.
Joseph is almost ready now,
and the road is very steep and slow."

Seventy miles to Bethlehem,
how sharp the stones beneath her feet.
"Dear Lady, climb upon my back,
and I will make your journey sweet."

Fifty miles to Bethlehem,
traveling in the starlit night.
"Little donkey, did you know
you carry God's own Son tonight?"

Thirty miles to Bethlehem,
still a long way from town.
"Dear Lady, will your little boy
have eyes like yours, so soft and brown?"

Ten more miles to Bethlehem.
Tiny creatures stop and stare.
Little donkey feels so proud
of the Holy Family in his care.

Through the gates of Bethlehem,
the end of the journey here at last.
Little donkey lifts his head.
What crowds of people walking past!

"No room! No room in Bethlehem!
Come to my stable, dark and warm.
Your little baby will not mind.
It's here he's chosen to be born."

NATHAN'S PRIDE

Nathan was a shepherd boy from Bethlehem.
The kids in town all made him feel ashamed.
They'd laugh and taunt, "Oh, shepherd boy,
you can't even read or write your name."

Nathan prayed that God would make him different,
for being "just a shepherd" made him sad.
"Be proud of who you are," his father told him,
"our great King David was also a shepherd lad."

One starry night when all the town was sleeping
and the sheep were sleeping, standing statue-still,
a sudden blinding light awakened Nathan;
and an angel song he heard upon the hill.

The angels sang a song of peace and blessings
and told about the infant born that night.
Nathan and his father hurried into town
to see if they could find that holy sight.

When the baby in the manger smiled at Nathan,
Nathan's face glowed like a Christmas tree.
"To be just a simple shepherd must be special,
for this tiny babe from heaven smiled at me!"

The babe in the manger cooed happily.
His tiny arms flew open wide.
And the little lamb felt safe and warm,
nestled there at the baby's side.

When the Holy Family left that place
to journey to their strange new home,
Mary took the lamb along
as a playmate for her infant Son.

The little lamb grew, and the boy did too,
as they romped in the hills of Galilee.
And Mary knew as she watched
those two what a loving Good Shepherd
her Jesus would be.

SECRETS OF
THAT FIRST CHRISTMAS

The shepherds knew on the first Christmas morn,
when angels sang on their quiet hill,
that a Savior had come to Bethlehem town
to bring peace to people of goodwill.

BUT THEY DIDN'T KNOW WHAT WE KNOW!

That the little child with the gentle smile
was really God's very own Son.
That he'd tell the world of his Father's love.
That through him would heaven be won.

THE MESSAGE OF THE STAR

In the little town of Bethlehem,
a special child of love was born.
As crickets chirped and people slept,
God gave the world his only Son.

Some Wise Men from a distant land
were filled with silent wondering.
For in the velvet sky of night,
one brilliant star was beckoning.

The message of that star was clear.
Somewhere a king was born that night.
So the Wise Men, packing their finest gifts,
set out to follow the heavenly light.

They kept their eyes upon the skies,
across mountains high and deserts wide.
They spoke of wondrous things to come,
with the star as their ever-constant guide.

Then, at long last, the star came to rest
above the sleepy town of Bethlehem.
They found the infant King they sought,
and they knelt in prayer to honor him.

The starlit message of that holy eve
echoes in the air each Christmas night.
Jesus is our King, ruler of our hearts,
light of our world, and source of our delight.

TRIM THE TREE FOR JESUS

It's time to trim the tree again
with sparkling tinsel and twinkling lights.
Hang a little angel there for Mary
to bring her good news this night.

It's time to trim the tree again
with icicles and silver bells.
Hang a donkey there for Joseph
to carry Mary over the hills.

It's time to trim the tree again,
soft cotton snow upon each limb.
Here's a little lamb from the shepherds,
a wooly gift to comfort him.

It's time to trim the tree again
with candy canes and
    gingerbread men.
Hang a star to guide the Magi
    across the miles to Bethlehem.

It's time to trim the tree again
with cranberry chains and
    popcorn balls. Bring your heart
        as a Christmas gift for the Babe
        who brings joy to us all.

MY FAMILY'S CHRISTMAS STABLE

My very favorite Christmas scene
is on our best parlor table.
There on a cloth of sparkling
green stands our family
Christmas stable.

I love to take the tiny folks
and move them left to right
until Christmas day starts happening
once again for my delight.

Here are the Wise Men
journeying.
Here are the shepherds
on the hill.
Here the animals
crowd around
(even the cow is
hushed and still).

Last comes the
Holy Family
and the tiny baby
born this day.
Then when all are
in their place,
here is the prayer
I say…

PRAYER BEFORE THE CHRISTMAS CRIB

Baby on the soft warm hay,
I have a birthday gift for you.
I'm wrapping up this whole, long day,
all filled with good things I can do.

I'll help my parents
in the house
and try hard to obey.
I'll do a kind deed
for my friend,
and I'll be cheerful
when we play.

I'll clean my plate at every meal.
I'll put my toys and games away.
I'll go to bed without a fuss
and kneel down silently to pray.

Baby on the soft warm hay,
how do you like
my gift today?

THAT'S WHAT CHRISTMAS IS FOR

Many, many years ago
there was no such thing
as Christmas day.
Everyone was terribly sad
because God the Father lived far away.

BUT...

Really, he was quite close by
planning an extra special way
to redeem (that means *save)*
the people he loved
and keep his promise of another day.
"You are my people," God's promise began,
"and I will be near whenever you pray."

Cherishing (that means *loving*) us so,
God did the most wonderful thing he could do.
He gave us his own beloved Son,
who was born as a child exactly like you
and raised in a family a lot like yours,
with Mary, his mother, and Saint Joseph too.

If God had not given the gift of his Son
to be born to Mary on the first Christmas day,
showing us all how much we are loved,
then heaven would still seem far, far away.

So maybe the very best present to give
would be like the one God gave from the start.
A love-gift that comes with a hug and a prayer
and a promise to love everyone every day,
something that even the littlest child
can wrap up in kindness and then give away.

MERRY CHRISTMAS